How Germs Spread

by Rod Barkman

Minneapolis, Minnesota

Credits
All images are courtesy of Shutterstock.com, unless otherwise specified. With thanks to Getty Images, Thinkstock Photo, and iStockphoto.
Cover – yusufdemirci. Recurring – robuart, Anatolir, ONYXprj. 5 – klyaksun. 6–7 – sveta, zuki70, arcyto. 8 – Tartila. 12 – ploypilin. 13 – Prostock-Studio. 14 – ONYXprj. 15 – mejnak, Sudowoodo, Jukkrapun Thipsupa. 16 – ONYXprj. 17 – alazur, Macrovector, ONYXprj, FG Trade. 18 – LerinaInk, nanskyblack. 19 – DGKylee. 20 – yusufdemirci. 21 – hvostik, Maridav. 22 – Sylfida. 23 – solar22.

Library of Congress Cataloging-in-Publication Data is available at www.loc.gov or upon request from the publisher.

ISBN: 979-8-88916-972-7 (hardcover)
ISBN: 979-8-89232-494-6 (paperback)
ISBN: 979-8-89232-134-1 (ebook)

Bearport Publishing is a division of Chrysalis Education Group.

For more information, write to Bearport Publishing, 5357 Penn Avenue South, Minneapolis, MN 55419.

Contents

Too Small to See

Think of the smallest thing you can see. What is it? Can you imagine something even smaller?

Germs are so itty-bitty that we can't see them with our eyes alone. Yet, they are everywhere around us!

Meet the Germs

Let's meet three main types of germs.

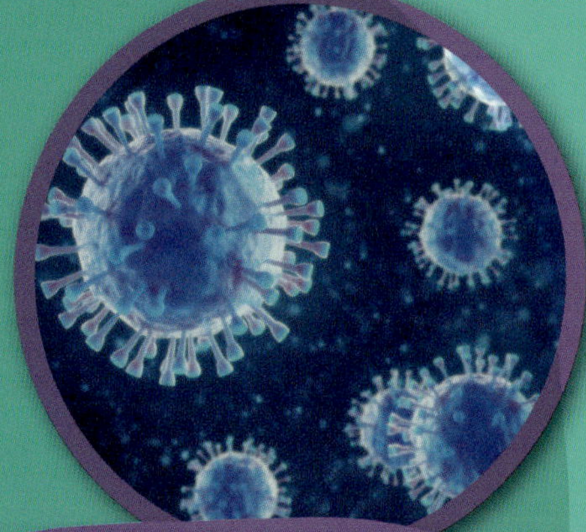

Hello, I'm a **virus**. Stay back, or you might get sick!

Howdy! I'm a **fungus**. Some fungi are small like me, but my mushroom friends are huge!
Hello! I'm a **bacterium** (bak-TEER-ee-uhm). Most of my bacteria friends are good, but some are bad.

All over the Place

These little germs are everywhere around us. Some are on top of our desks. Others are on the door handles we touch. Anything you can think of probably has germs on it!

Don't worry, though. You can still touch most things.
Many of the germs around us are actually harmless. They never cause you problems.
You're safe with us!

Feeling Unwell

What about the not-so-good germs? If those icky germs get into our bodies, they can make us feel sick.

Germs can make you sneeze or have a runny nose. Some can make your **stomach** upset. They may even make your skin feel itchy.

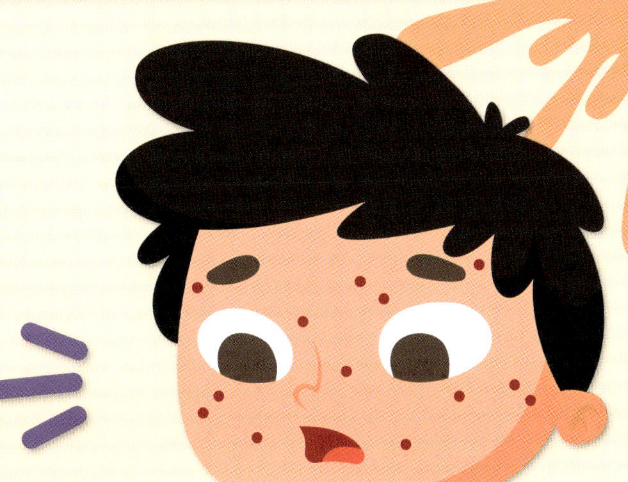

A rash caused by chicken pox

Have you heard of **chicken pox**? Sorry, one of my virus friends causes that!

In the Air

There are many different ways germs can spread. One way is through the air that we breathe. When we take air into and push it out of our bodies, we also breathe germs in and out.

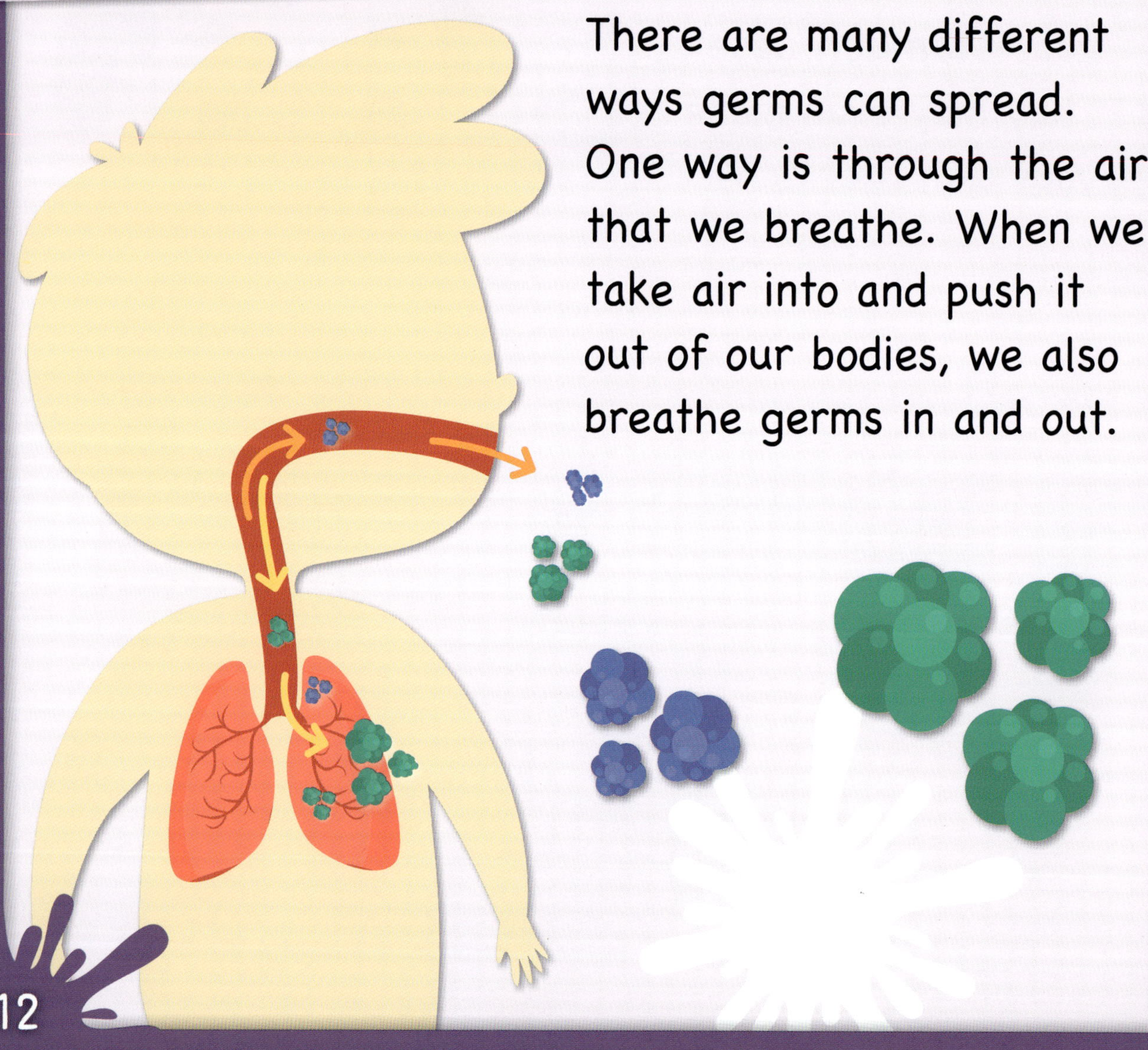

This is because germs can get into the air after we cough or sneeze. One big sneeze can shoot out germs not only from our mouths but also from our noses.

On Surfaces

Once germs are in the air, they can travel far and wide. Some land on **surfaces**, or the outer layers of things we touch. They might get on a nearby table or a faraway chair.

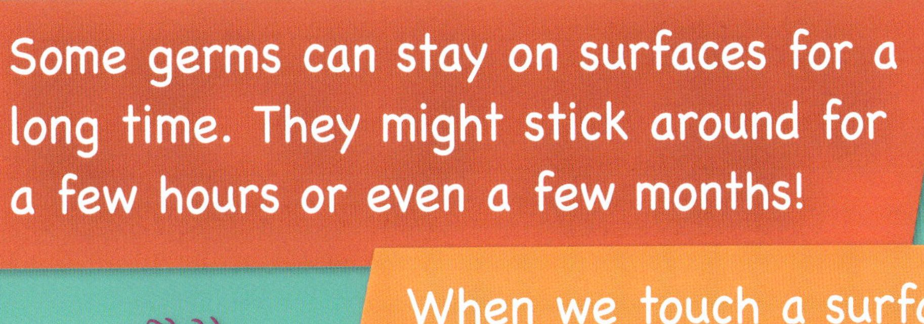

Some germs can stay on surfaces for a long time. They might stick around for a few hours or even a few months!

When we touch a surface, the germs move onto our hands.

In Water

Another way that germs can spread is in water. Luckily, many places clean the water before it gets to our taps. This makes it safe to drink.

Chemicals help stop germs from spreading in water. Swimming pools are full of a chemical called chlorine (KLOR-een). It helps get rid of almost all the germs in the water.

Now the water is clean and safe to swim in!

By Touch

Germs are easily passed around from our hands and to other people. They spread very quickly.

High fives and handshakes are just some of the many ways germs spread by touch.

We use our hands for a lot of things, including rubbing our eyes and eating our food. If we have germs on our hands when we do these things, the germs end up inside our bodies.

Stop the Spread

We can stop germs from spreading with some simple tricks. Let's learn a few of them!

Wash Up

Wash your hands in warm water using lots of soap. Rub your hands for 20 seconds to get rid of bad germs.

Wipe Surfaces

Wiping down surfaces before you use them helps get rid of most of the bacteria living on them.

Grab a Tissue

Cover your mouth and nose with a tissue before you sneeze. This helps stop germs from getting into the air.

Not All Bad

Keeping away bad germs lets good ones do their thing!

Medicine

Some germs can be made into **vaccines** (vak-SEENZ). Vaccines help protect us against **diseases**.

Doctors can give us vaccines through shots.

Gut Bacteria

The bacteria in our **intestines** help us break down food. This keeps our bodies running smoothly.

Intestines

The germs around us are small, but they help us in many ways!

Glossary

bacterium a tiny living thing that can make you sick or keep you healthy

chemicals substances that are made by scientists

chicken pox a type of illness that causes itchy, red spots on the skin

diseases illnesses that cause harm to the health of plants, animals, or people

fungus a plantlike living thing that can't make its own food

intestines the lower part of the digestive system that helps break down food

stomach a part of the body that breaks down food you eat

surfaces outside parts or layers of things, such as the tops of tables

vaccines medicines that protect people against diseases

virus a tiny germ that can make our bodies sick

Index